The Middle East

IRAQ
THEN AND NOW

John King

Chicago, Illinois

MONKEY PUZZLE MEDIA LTD

Produced for Raintree by
Monkey Puzzle Media Ltd.
Gissing's Farm, Fressingfield
Suffolk IP21 5SH, UK

For information, address the publisher:
Raintree, 100 N. LaSalle, Suite 1200,
Chicago, IL 60602
Customer Service 888-363-4266
Visit our website at www.raintreelibrary.com

Printed and bound in China by South China
Printing Company Ltd

10 09 08 07 06
10 9 8 7 6 5 4 3 2 1

Edited by Jenny Siklós and Paul Mason
Designed by Tim Mayer
Picture Research by Lynda Lines and Frances Bailey
Production by Duncan Gilbert
The consultant, Dr. Robert Stern, works as a part-time
analyst for the State Department, primarily as part of
the War on Terror. He is a former Associate Director
for Counter-Terrorism.

**Library of Congress Cataloging-in-Publication
Data**
King, John, 1939–
    Iraq then and now / John King
        p. : maps ; cm. -- (The Middle East)
    Includes bibliographical references and index.
    ISBN 1-4109-1622-7 (hc) -- ISBN 1-4109-1628-6 (pb)
    1. Iraq--History--1921---Juvenile literature.
    I. Title. II. Series.

DS79.K54 2005
956.704--dc22

2005002951

Acknowledgments
The author and publisher are grateful to the
following for permission to reproduce copyright
material: AKG-Images p. **10** (Visioars); Camera
Press pp. **18**, **22** (Reza), **27** (Mohamed Ansar),
37 (Tina Paul); Corbis pp. **6** (Chris Ison/Reuters),
12 (Bettmann), **13** (Bettmann), **14** (Hulton-
Deutsch Collection), **23** (Ed Kashi), **26**, **30** (Les
Stone), **34** (Sean Adair/Reuters), **36** (Ray
Stubblebine/ Reuters), **43** (Ali Abu Shish), **47**
(Faleh Kheiber/Reuters); Empics pp. **3** (EPA), **33**
(EPA); Getty Images pp. **17** (Central Press), **19**
(AFP), **32** (Karim Sahib/AFP), **40** (Mauricio Lima),
46 (Wathiq Khuzaie); Popperfoto.com p. **15**;
Reuters pp. **4** (Steven Pearsall), **9** (Suhaib Salem),
39 (Zohra Bensemra), **45** (Thaier Al-Sudani); Rex
Features pp. **5** bottom (SIPA), **20** (SIPA), **21**
(SIPA), **24** (SIPA), **29** (SIPA), **35** (SIPA), **38**
(Eddie Mulholland/EMU), **41** (Lena Kara), **44**
(Ron Sachs/CNP); Topfoto pp. **16**, **25**, **28** (Roger
Viollet); Werner Forman Archive p. **7** (British
Museum, London).

Cover photograph shows Iraqi Shi'ite Muslims
throwing stones at the head of a broken statue of
Saddam Hussein in Sadr City, Baghdad, December
2003 (Getty Images/Ahmad Al-Rubaye).

Map illustrations by Encompass Graphics Ltd.

Every effort has been made to contact copyright
holders of any material reproduced in this book.
Any omissions will be rectified in subsequent
printings if notice is given to the publishers.

The paper used to print this book comes from
sustainable resources.

Contents

Some words are shown in **bold**, like this. You can find out what they mean by looking in the Glossary.

"We Got Him!"

"We got him!" These were the words of Paul Bremer, the U.S. Administrator in Iraq, who announced the capture of former Iraqi president Saddam Hussein, at a press conference on the afternoon of Sunday, December 14, 2003.

General Ricardo Sanchez, Commander of the U.S. forces in Iraq (left), and Paul Bremer, announcing the capture of Saddam.

Since becoming the ruler of Iraq in 1979, Saddam Hussein had been cruel and brutal. He was captured in the town of al-Dawr, not far from Tikrit, on the evening of Saturday, December 13, 2003. Tikrit was Saddam Hussein's place of birth and had been the center of his family's power. The former Iraqi **dictator**, who had once lived in a palace, was hiding in a concealed cellar near a farmer's shack. He had food, clothing, and money, but was unshaven and confused. Though armed, he did not resist arrest.

The United States and its allies went to war against Saddam's Iraq in March 2003. Iraq was known to have had **chemical weapons**, and possibly also **biological weapons**, in 1991. It also had the beginnings of a nuclear weapons program. In 2003 the United States and Great Britain believed action was necessary because they thought Saddam Hussein had been refusing to obey earlier **United Nations** resolutions. The resolutions demanded that he get rid of his **weapons of mass destruction**.

❝ He was cowering in a hole in the ground. In the last analysis, he seemed not terribly brave. ❞
(Donald Rumsfeld, U.S. Secretary of Defense)

The invasion of Iraq began on March 20 with a major air attack on the Iraqi capital, Baghdad. At the same time, American and British troops moved into the south of the country, fighting their way north toward Baghdad. The invasion of Iraq was soon completed. American troops captured Baghdad on April 9, and on May 1, President Bush declared that the war was over. Though the United States hoped resistance would end with the capture of Saddam Hussein, this did not happen. Violence in Iraq continued. The puzzle was, how had Iraq's past led it to such a confrontation?

SADDAM'S WAR

Saddam Hussein defied the United Nations and the United States from the time of his invasion of Kuwait in 1991 up to 2003, when his regime was finally overthrown. United Nation sanctions had reduced Iraq to poverty. Iraq was allowed to sell oil for food, and 80 percent of the population depended on this. But some of the money did not go to the ordinary Iraqis. Instead it went to Saddam and his associates. When the United States-led invasion began, many Iraqis were relieved, hoping for an end to dictatorship and for a return of prosperity.

Iraq, its oil installations, and its neighbors. Iraq's oil is crucial to the country's economy and the main reason for its importance in the Middle East.

U.S. Marines taking up position on the outskirts of Baghdad, April 7, 2003.

The First Civilizations

Iraq lies in the ancient land known as **Mesopotamia**, which is the site of some of the earliest human settlements. Two great rivers, the Euphrates and Tigris, run through this land.

The culture of Sumer flourished in Mesopotamia 5,000 years ago, making it one of the world's oldest civilizations. The people of Sumer invented ways of **irrigating** their land, built brick houses, and kept written records. They also began to study science, mathematics, and astronomy.

Another achievement in early Mesopotamia was the writing of the first epic poems. The *Book of Gilgamesh*, dating from this time, tells the story of a legendary king who fought to preserve his city. Other poems were about the world's origins, and how the world was created by the gods.

> **❝ What a country can accomplish in the modern world is founded on its achievements in history. ❞**
> *(Ra'id Abdul Ridha Mohammed, Iraqi archaeologist)*

Iraqi fisherman on the Euphrates River. Traditional skills such as fishing have changed little since ancient times.

An ancient Sumerian wooden panel, made in around 2500 B.C.E., showing a banquet. The picture shows how the rulers of Sumer lived, 4,500 years ago.

Iraq is also the site of the city of Babylon, which is mentioned in the Bible, and is believed to have been built almost 4,000 years ago. Soon after, the region's King Hammurabi was the first to write down a system of laws. Later, about 2,500 years ago, another king, Nebuchadnezzar, built the Hanging Gardens of Babylon, one of the Seven Wonders of the Ancient World.

The land of Iraq next became part of the Empire of Persia, whose rulers lived to the east, in what is today Iran. In 331 B.C.E. Alexander the Great conquered the country for the Greeks. Two hundred years later, the Persians recaptured Iraq. Persian rule continued until 636 C.E., when Arab invaders arrived.

" Babylon was the capital of the world and the source of all the laws of humankind. "
(Saheb El-Doulaimy, a guide at the site of the ancient city)

ANCIENT TRADITIONS
"How many of us realize that if we fear bad luck when we see a black cat, or count time in 12 hours for each day and night, or look up at the stars to read our fortune in the constellations, it was the civilization of ancient Iraq which invented all these things?"
(Leonard Woolley, archaeologist)

Islam Comes to Iraq

The Prophet Mohammed, the founder of the Muslim religion, died in 632 C.E. In the years after his death, the Arabs burst out of Arabia and overran the lands known today as the Middle East, including Iraq. Muslim Arabs first defeated the Persian rulers of Iraq in 637 C.E.

This key 637 C.E. battle between Persians and Muslim Arabs took place at Qadisiyah, on the Euphrates River. This is near the modern Iraqi city of Najaf. The Arabs defeated a Persian army led by an Iranian prince called Rustam.

The Umayyad Empire, 661–750 C.E.

Empire extent

The Umayyads were a dynasty of Arabian Muslim Caliphs who ruled an empire stretching from Spain to India. They came to power in 661 C.E., following the death of the Prophet Mohammed's cousin Ali (see page 9). In 750 C.E. they were overthrown by the Abbasids.

In 656 C.E., an argument over who should lead Islam broke out among the Muslims in Arabia. Ali, the Prophet Mohammed's cousin and son-in-law, believed he had the right to be leader, or **Caliph**, of the Muslims. Ali was recognized as Caliph in Iraq and Persia (modern Iran). But the Muslim rulers in Damascus chose another successor, Mu'awiya ibn Abi Sufyan. This led to a great division among Muslims, with the creation of two groups, the Shi'a, or **Shi'ite Muslims**, and the **Sunni Muslims**. The Shi'a, or the "faction," followed Ali. The Sunni Muslims, who claimed they were following the customs laid down by Mohammed, backed Mu'awiya and the Caliphs who followed him.

In 661 C.E. Ali was murdered in the Iraqi city of Kufa, to the rage and despair of the Shi'a. In the coming centuries, the majority of Arabs would be Sunni Muslims, while the Shi'ite faith was mainly found among the Arabs of southern Iraq. Neighboring non-Arab Iran also became almost entirely Shi'ite.

About 100 years later, the city of Baghdad was founded where the two great rivers, the Tigris and the Euphrates, meet. Baghdad became the capital of what is now Iraq. The region, and especially Baghdad itself, became the capital of the **Abbasid dynasty** and a great center of Arabic culture, power, and wealth.

The Abbasid Mosque at Samarra was built in 852 C.E. When it was built, it was one of the largest mosques in the Islamic world.

THE SHI'ITE MUSLIMS

Today, there are many Shi'ites in southern Iraq, and they form 60 percent of the country's total population. Neighboring Iran is a Shi'ite country. Ali is buried in the Iraqi city of Najaf.

Mongols, Kurds, and Turks

During the 1200s Iraq was conquered by the Mongols, a tribal people from deep inside Asia. The Mongols swept westward, mercilessly conquering and destroying all that lay in their path. Their chief, Hulagu, the grandson of Genghis Khan, seized Baghdad in 1258.

> **Again and again, almost the entire [population] of a city was massacred ... the terror was unprecedented.**
> (Marshall C. Hodgson, a modern historian, describing the Mongol invasion)

When the Mongols arrived, most Iraqis regarded themselves as Arabs and spoke Arabic. The separate culture of the **Kurds** had survived, however, along with other smaller cultural groups. Some Iraqis even continued to practice the Christian faith. These **minorities** are still present in 21st-century Iraq.

The Kurds, who lived in northern Iraq, also lived in neighboring areas of Iran and Turkey. They spoke their own language, and regarded themselves as a separate people from the Arabs. They are mostly Sunni Muslims, though some are Shi'ites.

This illustration shows the siege of Baghdad by the Mongol army in 1258 C.E. Hulagu, who led the army, warned the Caliph that he must surrender or his city and his land would be burned.

The Kurds are still culturally separate today, and many would like independence and their own country.

The Mongols were not Muslims, but soon converted to Islam. Over the coming centuries, power in the region was disputed between the Mongol chieftains, Persian princes, and Turkish warlords who had also originally come from the east.

The Ottoman Turks captured Baghdad in 1534. For the next three hundred years, local leaders opposed Turkish rule. But by 1834, the Ottoman Turks had gained control of the region that became the three **provinces** of Mosul, Baghdad, and Basra, on the fringe of the **Ottoman Empire**.

THE OTTOMAN EMPIRE

The Ottoman Empire began in one of the Turkish states that sprang up in Anatolia (today the Asian part of modern Turkey). In 1453 C.E. the Ottomans conquered Byzantium, the last remaining part of the Roman Empire, and launched attacks on Europe. The Ottoman Turks adopted **Constantinople** as their capital, and renamed it Istanbul. The Ottomans dominated the Middle East for almost four centuries.

> **❝** These are lands great in extent, important by their position, once marvellously wealthy, and still potentially so. **❞**
> *(Stephen Longrigg, a modern historian, writing about Iraq)*

0   50   100   150 miles
0   80   160   240 km

N

Tigris

MOSUL

Euphrates

Syrian Desert

Baghdad

Tigris

BAGHDAD

Mesopotamia

Euphrates

Tigris

BASRA

Ottoman Provinces
.... Late 19th-century admin boundaries
——— Modern international borders

This map shows the Ottoman Provinces of Mosul, Baghdad, and Basra, and the location of the city of Baghdad.

1921: Britain Creates The Kingdom of Iraq

In the early days of the 20th century, Arab **nationalists** within the Turkish-ruled Ottoman Empire began to believe that the Arabs had a right to live in countries of their own. The coming of World War I, which lasted from 1914 to 1918, gave the Arabs their chance, after the Turks decided to fight on Germany's side.

The British encouraged the Arab tribes of Arabia to revolt against the Turks and promised to help all the Arabs when the war was over. But at the same time, Great Britain and France secretly agreed to divide up the whole of the Middle East into zones that they would control. Iraq was to be controlled by Britain.

Baghdad in 1920, after a revolt against British rule.

Emir Faisal (later King of Iraq) in 1919. Behind him on the right stands T.E. Lawrence, the British Army officer who fought in the Arab revolt with the Arabs.

> **"** There is still no Iraqi people, only masses lacking any patriotic ideal, connected by no common tie, prone to anarchy, and always ready to rise up against any government whatsoever. **"**
>
> (King Faisal of Iraq explains the problems of ruling the country)

THE HASHEMITES

The Hashemite family of Mecca had for centuries held the post of Governor of Mecca under the Ottoman Turks. The head of the family during World War I was Sharif Hussein. His sons Faisal and Abdullah led the Arab revolt against the Turks. Faisal later became king of Iraq. Major T.E. Lawrence, who became known as "Lawrence of Arabia," was the British officer sent to help organize the revolt.

After the war, the League of Nations, the international body set up by the winners of World War I to keep the peace, asked Britain to supervise Iraq and lead it to independence. This was known as the British **Mandate**. However the population was made up of many different peoples, and Iraq was difficult to rule. In particular the Kurds in the northern province of Mosul wanted to be part of a separate country.

Britain decided Iraq would be more stable with a king. In 1921 the British chose King Faisal, from the family that had led the Arab revolt against the Turks. Meanwhile, the search for oil, which had begun before World War I, led to discoveries of large quantities in 1927.

The Monarchy 1921-1958

King Faisal was at first little known in Iraq. The British appointed Arab officials to run the country. Some were former Ottoman officials and others were Arab nationalists. Most were Sunni Muslims, despite the fact that most Iraqis were Shi'ites. Great Britain also chose an assembly to draft a **constitution**. British advisers played an important role.

In 1924 Iraq became a constitutional monarchy, where the king and an elected parliament each played a part. Treaties between Iraq and Britain ensured that the British continued to have a strong influence. In 1932 Iraq became independent, though the British continued to rule behind the scenes.

King Faisal died in 1933 and was succeeded by King Ghazi, who died in a car accident in 1939. His heir, King Faisal II, was only four years old, so a **regent** ruled on his behalf. In 1941, during World War II, politicians sympathetic to Nazi Germany rebelled. They formed a new government and appointed a different ruler. British forces quickly restored the former **regime**.

King Faisal II in 1945, when he was ten years old. He became king when he was four years old, and Iraq was ruled by a regent until Faisal II became eighteen.

14

After the war, Arab nationalists objected to Britain's attempt to negotiate a new treaty with Iraq. They also protested in 1955 against the pro-Western Baghdad Pact (see the panel on the right). Then, in 1958, to the surprise of the politicians and the royal family, there was a violent military **coup** led by General Qassem, a nationalist sympathetic to Egypt's President Nasser. Monarchy in Iraq came to a sudden and bloody end.

> ❝ The Arabs have shown that they are united in their aims, despite imperialist attempts to sow [disagreement] among them. ❞
> (Al-Ahram *newspaper, recalling the views of Egypt's President Nasser on the coup in Iraq*)

THE BAGHDAD PACT

The Baghdad Pact, as it became known, took shape in 1955, when Iraq signed a defense agreement with Turkey. Iran and Pakistan also joined the Pact, of which Britain was a leading member. The aim was to establish a defense system that would strengthen the Middle East against communist influence. Iraq left the Baghdad Pact in 1959, after the 1958 revolution.

Iraq's Prime Minister Nuri al-Said speaks to the press before a meeting of the Baghdad Pact Council in April 1956.

Military Regimes 1958-1968

General Qassem, who seized power on July 14, 1958. He believed the monarchy had not been in the interests of ordinary Iraqis.

In the Qassem coup of 1958, the King and a number of leading politicians, including Prime Minister Nuri al-Said, were killed. This brutality was new to Iraqi politics. General Qassem also had ruthless rivals. In 1959 a **Ba'athist** group tried to murder him, but failed. One of the would-be assassins was the young Saddam Hussein, who later had to flee the country.

Soon after gaining power, Qassem came into conflict with the West. In 1961 he stopped the British-owned Iraq Petroleum Company exploring for oil. He then set up the Iraqi National Oil Company. Qassem also took land from the big landowners to give to the poor farm workers. In 1961 Qassem claimed Kuwait was historically part of Iraq (see page 25). Great Britain took this threat seriously, and moved British troops into Kuwait for its protection. Qassem also alarmed the West by starting a friendly relationship with the Soviet Union, which gave Iraq weapons.

> ❝ Our revolution was not an accident: it was the outcome of careful planning and was based on Iraq's political needs. ❞
> (*General Qassem, 1958*)

> **“** How can a united nation be built, except by fierce struggle. Every Arab must seek in his heart to find the right way forward. **”**
> *(Ba'ath Party statement on how Arab peoples might be united)*

Soldiers and tanks in Baghdad following the Ba'athist overthrow of General Qassem.

In 1963 a group of anti-communist army officers, who were members of the **Ba'ath Party**, succeeded in overthrowing Qassem. However the new president, Abdel-Salam Arif, soon left the Ba'ath Party. He then took personal control, and resumed links with Moscow. In 1968 yet another military coup brought the Ba'athists back to power, and President Hassan Bakr became leader of a new Ba'athist government.

THE BA'ATH PARTY

The Ba'ath Party was founded in Syria in the 1940s by Michael Aflaq and Salaheddin Bitar. The Arabic word Ba'ath means "rebirth." The party's aim is to achieve freedom and unity for the Arabs. There are groups of Ba'athists throughout the Arab world. The party came to power in Iraq, and also in Syria. Though the Ba'ath Party believes in **democracy** in theory, all Ba'athist rulers have been dictators.

President Bakr and the Ba'ath Party would rule Iraq for many years. Bakr's right-hand man was Saddam Hussein, whose role was to ensure that there would be no resistance to the regime. Saddam was the organizer and enforcer as the Ba'ath eliminated its opponents, executing or imprisoning all who might be a danger to it.

In 1972 Iraq took control of the foreign-owned Iraq Petroleum Company; in 1973 it would take complete control of its oil resources. Iraq was beginning to be a major oil producer. In 1972 the Ba'athists, who had opposed communism, signed a friendship treaty with the communist Soviet Union.

From 1973 onward, Iraq was basically a dictatorship. The Ba'ath Party promised that democracy would eventually be restored, but this never happened. Membership of the Party grew. An increase in oil prices in 1973 gave Iraq an increased income, and Iraq began to prosper and flourish as a modern state.

IRAQ AND THE SOVIET UNION

The 1972 Treaty of Friendship with the Soviet Union meant Iraq got military and technical help from Moscow. At the time, the Soviet Union and the United States were engaged in the Cold War, a long period of antagonism. Choosing to side with the Soviet communists meant Iraq lost the sympathy of the United States.

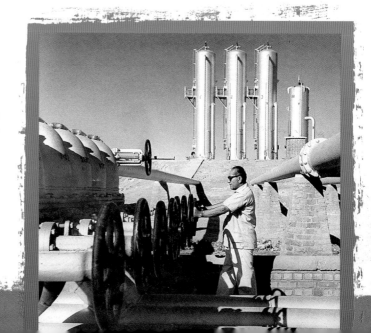

Iraqi oil installations at Kirkuk in 1972. The country's oil industry was fully nationalized in 1973.

Despite the increased prosperity, there were troubles in northern Iraq, where the Kurds had never given up their ambition to have their own separate state. Many Kurds continued to want an independent country, called Kurdistan. In 1974 there was open war between the Kurds and the Baghdad government. Neither side won outright, and the resentment of the Kurds continued.

By the mid-1970s, President Bakr's health was not good. He began to withdraw from the leadership, as Saddam Hussein took greater control. Saddam began to increase his power by giving key positions to members of his family. He also appointed officials with whom he had tribal links, or a shared origin in the town of Tikrit. By 1977 most officials reported to Saddam Hussein. On July 16, 1979, Bakr resigned and Saddam Hussein took his place as president of Iraq.

This photograph, taken in 1976, shows then Vice President Saddam Hussein (seated on the left) with President Ahmed Hassan Bakr to the right.

ff Iraq's former treaty with Great Britain was forced on the Iraqi people. Iraq's treaty with the Soviet Union is based on genuine shared interests. JJ

(Saddam Hussein, speaking in 1972)

Saddam as President

In 1979 Saddam Hussein became president of the Iraqi Republic, secretary-general of the Ba'ath Party, chairman of the **Revolutionary Command Council**, and commander-in-chief of Iraq's armed forces. He was in charge of a wealthy country. Iraq was not as rich as Saudi Arabia or Kuwait, but its oil revenues meant that everyone had jobs, while education and health services were free.

Saddam's first action was to eliminate all those who might oppose him. Five members of the 21-member Revolutionary Command Council were accused of treason and executed, along with 50 other senior leaders. Hundreds of junior officials were executed or dismissed.

Saddam Hussein also tried to attract popular support. He took a surprising step by deciding to restore Iraq's parliament, which had not met since 1958. However it was virtually impossible for anyone but a Ba'ath Party member to qualify to stand for membership of the new 250-member assembly, so the voters had little choice.

Saddam Hussein takes his place on the international scene. Here, in 1979, as Iraq's new president, he attends the summit of non-aligned nations in Havana, Cuba.

SADDAM HUSSEIN
Born on April 28, 1937, Saddam Hussein was brought up near the small town of Tikrit, raised by his uncle. In 1957 Saddam joined the Ba'ath Party and in 1959 took part in an attempt to murder Iraq's military ruler, General Qassem. He fled to Syria and then to Egypt, returning to Iraq in 1963 when the Ba'ath took power. He worked his way up through the ranks thanks to his closeness to Hassan Bakr, who became president in 1968.

Saddam also began to strengthen Iraq's army with all the modern arms he could get, some from the Soviet Union and some from the West. Iraq also began researching chemical and biological weapons. In addition Saddam pressed on with Iraq's nuclear research program, buying uranium fuel. Western experts said Iraq's nuclear plans could only be aimed at building nuclear bombs.

SADDAM'S BRUTALITY

Saddam Hussein became known for his brutality. He personally killed many political opponents. At the same time, he began to develop a taste for extravagance. He built vast palaces, with ornate decor and furniture, living a life of luxury.

ff With such a leader at its head, and with such wealth at its disposal, will Iraq now be able to revive its former glory? **JJ**
(Iraqi government statement on Saddam Hussein coming to power)

Iraq's military forces go on parade in Baghdad, under the triumphal arch of two swords designed by Saddam.

War with Iran

After Iran's Islamic Revolution of 1979, Saddam Hussein feared that Iran might stir up trouble in Iraq. Many Iraqis were Shi'ite Muslims, like the Iranians. They resented being ruled by Saddam's followers, who were mainly Sunni Muslims. Saddam also believed that so soon after the Islamic Revolution, Iran might be unprepared to defend itself.

Saddam wanted to seize the part of Iran next to Iraq, where many of the people spoke Arabic, and where Iran's oil resources were. He also wanted to get access to the entire waterway from Basra to the ocean, known as the Shatt el-Arab.

Iraqi troops attacked on September 2, 1980. Over the next eight years, war raged on. Iran surprised Iraq with the strength of its defense. Iranian troops crossed into Iraqi territory, and at one stage threatened the city of Basra. The two sides sank each other's ships in the Gulf, and aimed missiles at each other's cities. Saddam Hussein also attacked the Kurdish people inside Iraq, some of whom supported Iran.

Ayatollah Khomeini, the leader of Iran, speaks to his followers in Tehran in 1981.

> ❝ When they realized it was a chemical attack [the people] tried to get out, but most of them died in the shelters. ❞
> (Dana Nazif, a Kurdish resident of Halabja describes Saddam's attack on the city)

Kurdish fighters inspect a chemical bomb dropped from an Iraqi aircraft during the 1988 raid on Halabja.

The Arab states of the Gulf supported Iraq with loans and **subsidies** during the war. Iraq's own oil revenues suffered, and much of its remaining income was spent on the war. The West also supported Iraq. Arab and Western support was a result of fear that the Islamic Revolution in Iran might spread, threatening the existing governments in the region. From 1982 the United States and other Western countries gave economic support to Iraq, and supplied weapons and intelligence. In March 1908 Saddam Hussein ordered a chemical attack on Kurds in the northern Iraqi town of Halabja, killing 5,000 people. The United States expressed horror at the act at the time, but soon began to support Saddam Hussein once more.

The war did not go well for Iraq, and Saddam Hussein declared that it was over in August 1988. The major result of the war was that Iraq had sacrificed much of its former prosperity and was deeply in debt, especially to its oil-producing Arab neighbors, who had helped to fund the war.

SADDAM HUSSEIN AND WEAPONS OF MASS DESTRUCTION

Chemical weapons were developed by Iraq during the war with Iran, and were used against the Kurds and at the battlefront. Iraq also planned to develop biological weapons. But Saddam Hussein's big plan was to produce a nuclear weapon. This scheme was halted in June 1981, when Israeli warplanes destroyed Iraq's nuclear research reactor, "Osiraq," near Baghdad.

1990: The Invasion of Kuwait

After the end of the war with Iran, Saddam Hussein was furious with his Arab neighbors. He believed Iraq should not have to pay its debts, since Iraq had defended its neighbors from Iran. He also needed cash from Iraq's oil revenue, and accused Kuwait in particular of driving the oil price down by producing too much oil.

To the world's astonishment, Iraq invaded Kuwait in the early hours of the morning on August 2, 1990. (Saddam had previously said that he would *not* attack Kuwait.) There was little resistance. The ruler of Kuwait fled to Saudi Arabia. Iraq declared Kuwait to be its own territory. Saddam's plan was that Iraq would no longer need to pay its debt to Kuwait, and would have Kuwait's oil revenue for itself.

Only in the Arab world was there any support for Saddam Hussein. Some individual Arabs believed the Kuwaiti ruling family had been keeping oil money selfishly for their own use. Yemen and Sudan expressed support for Iraq, while Jordan remained neutral.

Iraqi tanks in Kuwait City on the morning of August 2, 1990.

August 29, 1990: refugees in Amman, Jordan. Refugees of all nationalities fled from Kuwait and Iraq after the war began.

In Washington, U.S. President George H.W. Bush announced he would not permit what he called "naked **aggression**." Other countries around the world also called on Iraq to withdraw. Up until 1990 the United States had not opposed Saddam Hussein, and he was surprised by the American reaction.

Some Kuwaitis who had fled the country made accusations that Iraqi troops had committed brutal attacks on the people while they held Kuwait. Most of these accusations were later found to be false. However homes and offices were looted, while the citizens of Kuwait were terrified and soon began to run short of food and other necessities.

IRAQ'S CLAIM TO KUWAIT

Kuwait was once part of the Ottoman province of Basra, which later became part of Iraq. In November 1914, after the outbreak of World War I, Great Britain recognized Kuwait as an independent state under British protection. But Saddam argued that Kuwait should have remained part of Iraq, like the rest of Basra Province. After the invasion he declared Kuwait to be Iraq's 19th province.

1991: Iraq Driven Out of Kuwait

The United States said its view on the Iraqi occupation of Kuwait was that international law must be observed, and no state may take the territory of another.

President George H.W. Bush persuaded many countries, including Great Britain and some Arab states, to join a military **coalition** to drive the Iraqis out. Many around the world believed the real issue was control of Kuwait's **oil reserves**. If Saddam had been able to combine the Kuwaiti oil reserves with those of Iraq, he would have been in control of a very large proportion of the world's oil.

> ❝ I will not allow this little dictator to control 25 percent of the civilized world's oil. ❞
> *(George H.W. Bush, speaking to King Hussein of Jordan, August 1990)*

U.S. President George H.W. Bush and the Commander of the allied forces, U.S. General Norman Schwarzkopf, in Saudi Arabia in November 1990.

Black smoke billows from a burning oil field in Kuwait, set alight by the fleeing Iraqi troops.

Saddam refused to withdraw his troops. In February 1991 the United States began a long bombardment of Iraqi positions in Kuwait and in Iraq itself. On February 24, 1991, the Coalition forces, under the command of U.S. General Norman Schwarzkopf, attacked the remaining Iraqi troops in Kuwait. The attack was called Operation Desert Storm. The Iraqis offered little resistance, but set Kuwait's oil wells on fire as they left. The United States estimated that 100,000 Iraqi troops were killed in the fighting.

A **ceasefire** was declared by the Coalition after four days. On March 3 the Iraqi military commanders accepted the terms put to them by the Coalition forces. The United States decided not to pursue the Iraqi troops back into Iraq. The reason given much later by the Coalition leadership was that if the Iraqi government were overthrown, it would be difficult to cope with the resulting situation in Iraq.

THE KURDS REBEL

After the Iraqi invasion of Kuwait, the Kurds of northern Iraq rose up against Saddam Hussein and declared themselves autonomous. Thousands of Kurds were killed by Iraqi forces and many fled. The UN then said there should be safe havens for the Kurds, and that the United States and Great Britain should protect them from Saddam Hussein. Under the protection of allied planes, the Kurds created an autonomous zone. In the south, however, no protection was given to the Shi'ites, and Saddam Hussein brutally suppressed a Shi'ite uprising.

1991-2001: Sanctions and the Effects

After the war the United Nations passed **Security Council Resolution** 687. This laid down rules for Iraq. Iraq had to respect the international frontier with Kuwait, give up its banned weapons, and pay compensation to Kuwait and other parties that had been harmed.

Though Iraq did not use chemical or biological weapons in the war over Kuwait, the fear remained that it possessed them. Security Council Resolution 687, passed in April 1991, said that Iraq could no longer trade until it got rid of its weapons of mass destruction and its missiles. Iraq was also supposed to pay compensation for damage done to Kuwait, and for losses of oil revenue. Until these conditions were met, Iraq was only allowed to import food and some other essentials. This meant that Iraq could no longer freely export oil and had little or no income.

UNITED NATIONS RESOLUTION 687

"Iraq must accept the destruction or removal of all nuclear material, chemical and biological weapons, and ballistic missiles with ranges greater than 93 miles (150 kilometers). The United Nations will monitor the destruction and removal of weapons."

A Baghdad hospital in April 1991. Sanctions made it difficult to care for Iraq's children.

Under the sanctions, Iraq's previously high standard of living dropped sharply. The country lost almost all oil income. The sanctions were modified when the United Nations set up an Oil-for-Food Program in 1995. Under this plan, accepted by Iraq, the country could export oil to pay for food and medical supplies. The Oil-for-Food Program improved the situation for ordinary Iraqis, but some of the money was not spent on food and medicine for the Iraqi people. Food had to be rationed, and many Iraqis lost their jobs. **Inflation** also reduced the value of people's incomes. Children in particular suffered. The **child mortality rate** rose, and schools and hospitals found it difficult to keep going.

The sanctions had a serious effect on ordinary Iraqis. However many people also believe that the Iraqi government could have done more to help its people. Instead it spent too much of its money on Saddam Hussein's own projects and for military purposes.

❝ There is a human calamity going on in Iraq ... caused by U.S.-driven economic sanctions. ❞
(Dennis Halliday, former United Nations humanitarian coordinator in Iraq)

❝ Those who believed in sanctions underestimated the Iraqi will to resist. ❞
(Paul D. Taylor, U.S. Naval War College)

Sajjud Palace, Baghdad, one of Saddam's many palaces.

29

1991-2002: The No-fly Zones

During the period from 1991 onward, "no-fly zones" were established over northern and southern Iraq. Iraqi planes were forbidden to fly and help Iraq's forces attack the Kurds or Shi'ites from the air. This operation was carried out by the United States and Britain, not the United Nations.

The no-fly zones were policed by American and British planes. They flew from bases in Turkey in the north and from aircraft carriers in the Gulf in the south. Iraqi planes were not allowed to fly south of the **latitude** 33 degrees north (which cuts across Iraq just south of Baghdad) or north of the latitude 36 degrees north. The operation was given the title "Provide Comfort."

The no-fly zones were intended to protect those parts of Iraq's population that had mounted uprisings in 1991 after the U.S.-led coalition had driven the Iraqis from Kuwait. These people were vulnerable to attack by Saddam Hussein's forces.

The southern zone gave some protection to the Shi'ite population. Iraq was allowed to use helicopters, however, and it used these to suppress a Shi'ite uprising in 1991. In the north, the Kurds did better. The no-fly zone protected the Kurdish autonomous area set up after 1991, allowing the Kurds to establish a government of their own.

Kurdish "Peshmerga" fighters, meaning "Those who face death," in the Kurdish area of northern Iraq.

During the period from the end of the war to 1998, U.S. and British planes flying in the no-fly zones attacked Iraqi aircraft, and also radar stations on the ground. These attacks became more severe and happened more often after Iraq's announcement in 1998 that it would no longer recognize the existence of the zones, which it thought interfered with Iraq's national rights. After Operation Desert Fox in 1998 (see pages 32–33), Iraq began to fire missiles at U.S. and British planes in the zones, whose attacks on ground targets in the no-fly zones increased.

(see pages 32–33)

AUTONOMY FOR THE KURDS

In October 1991 the Iraqi Government voluntarily withdrew from the Kurdish region of the country. The Kurds were left to govern themselves. Elections were held in May 1992 to elect a Kurdish parliament, and the Kurdish area set up its own regional government.

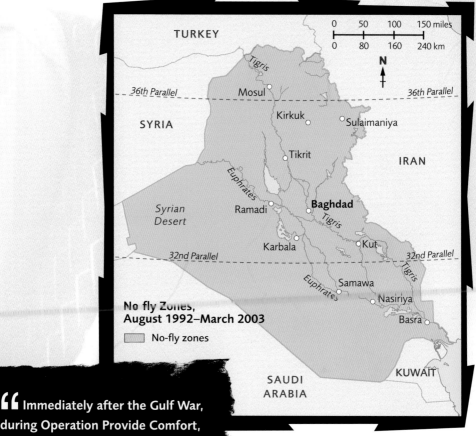

No fly Zones,
August 1992–March 2003

No-fly zones

" Immediately after the Gulf War, during Operation Provide Comfort, the goal was to protect the Kurds, but what we're doing now is enforcing the no-fly zone. **"**
(U.S.A.F. pilot)

This map shows the latitude lines, known as the 36th and 32nd parallels, that mark the northern and southern no-fly zones.

1991-2001: Sanctions and the Inspections

After Iraq's forces had been expelled from Kuwait, the United Nations sent in teams of weapons inspectors to check whether Saddam Hussein had destroyed his banned weapons. Despite much effort from the inspectors, no weapons of mass destruction were found.

In 1991 the United Nations had set up UNSCOM (United Nations Special Commission) to search Iraq for forbidden weapons. Saddam Hussein's officials gave UNSCOM little help. Saddam later claimed that he had disposed of his weapons of mass destruction in 1991, but did not wish to admit this as he thought it would make him appear weak in the eyes of his neighbors, especially Iran.

In 1998 Iraq completely stopped cooperating with UNSCOM after it refused to agree that there were no weapons. UNSCOM pulled out of Iraq. In December 1998 Iraq declared it would withdraw all cooperation unless the UN considered lifting the sanctions, adding that it would also cease to recognize the no-fly zones. In retaliation, U.S. President Bill Clinton launched four days of air attacks on Iraq. This was the start of what was known as Operation Desert Fox.

UN weapons inspectors set off under the watchful eyes of an Iraqi sentry in December 1998.

A UN resolution in December 1999 set up a new organization, UNMOVIC (United Nations Monitoring Inspection and Verification Commission). For three years Iraq refused to let UNMOVIC carry out inspections, changing its mind only in late 2002.

Before the invasion of Kuwait, Iraq certainly did have weapons of mass destruction. There have been suggestions that these may remain hidden, or could have been sent to another country. Most likely, they were destroyed as Saddam Hussein has claimed.

❝ If Saddam defies the world and we fail to respond, we will face a far greater threat in the future. **❞**
(U.S. President Clinton, speaking about Operation Desert Fox)

SADDAM HUSSEIN'S MURDEROUS REGIME

The United States has accused Saddam of killing 300,000 of his own citizens.

• **Roughly 180,000 Kurds died in 1988 when they were suspected of cooperating with Iran.**

• **At least 60,000 Shi'ites died when Saddam repressed their uprising against him in 1991.**

• **Another 60,000 people who died were political prisoners and others killed by Saddam's regime over the 25 years when he ran the country.**

Hundreds of thousands of Iraqis also died as soldiers in the Iraq-Iran war.

Inspectors of the UN organization UNSCOM prepare banned Iraqi missiles for destruction.

The World Trade Center, about to be hit by a second aircraft, during the September 11 attacks on the United States.

On September 11, 2001, hijacked aircraft destroyed the Twin Towers of the World Trade Center building in New York. The Pentagon was also hit, and one aircraft crashed in Pennsylvania. It is believed that the U.S. Capitol Building was the intended target of the Pennsylvania aircraft. The response of President George W. Bush was to call for a "War on Terror," though no target was immediately in view. Iraq was at first not mentioned.

On September 16 Vice President Dick Cheney said there was no evidence of any Iraqi involvement in the attacks. Instead responsibility was soon given to Osama bin Laden and his Al-Qaeda terrorist network. On October 3 Deputy Secretary of State Richard Armitage said that it was clear that bin Laden was to blame.

The United States reacted with an attack on Afghanistan, where bin Laden was based. On October 7 U.S. bombs began to fall on targets in that country. By December 2001, Afghan opposition forces had ousted the **Taliban** regime, which had supported Osama bin Laden. Bin Laden himself had disappeared from view, and U.S. special forces in Afghanistan failed to find him.

U.S. special forces in Afghanistan search mountain caves for Osama bin Laden in 2002.

In January 2002 President Bush made a speech that named Iraq, along with Iran and North Korea, as a member of what the President called an "Axis of Evil," because they were alleged to support terrorism. Throughout 2002 the United States continued to stress what it said was the danger to the world from Iraq.

On September 16, 2002, after President Bush's speech of September 12 to the United Nations (see page 36), Saddam Hussein suddenly invited the UN arms inspectors to return. UNMOVIC began work in November 2002. By this stage, however, it had begun to seem likely that President Bush's aim was to get rid of Saddam Hussein and replace his government with a different one. However, this was not yet official policy.

> **ff The United States certainly does not have the option of doing nothing about Saddam Hussein. JJ**
> (President George W. Bush's Secretary of State and former national security adviser, Condoleeza Rice)

THE NEO-CONSERVATIVES AND IRAQ

Among President Bush's policy advisers was a group known as the neo-conservatives. These advisers supported a U.S. foreign policy of bringing change to parts of the world hostile to the United States by installing pro-Western, democratic governments.

Iraq and the United Nations

One way in which the United States stepped up the pressure on Iraq was through the United Nations. President Bush spoke to the UN General Assembly on September 12, 2002. He accused Iraq of failing to comply with UN Security Council resolutions and of supporting terrorism. However he did not accuse Saddam Hussein directly of any part in the September 11 attacks.

On November 8, 2002, the UN Security Council passed Resolution 1441 condemning Iraq's failure to comply with previous resolutions. The United States and Great Britain had managed to get the approval of the other permanent members of the Security Council.

President George W. Bush addressing the UN General Assembly on September 12, 2002.

INTERNATIONAL ATTITUDES TO IRAQ

In Europe some governments supported President Bush's aims in Iraq. In Britain, Prime Minister Tony Blair agreed that British troops would join any invasion force. But many ordinary people disagreed and there were huge demonstrations against the war, in both Britain and the United States. Other countries, notably France, opposed the United States. Most Arab countries also opposed the invasion of Iraq.

An anti-war demonstration in New York's Central Park on October 6, 2002.

> 66 France is not anti-American. But we just feel that there is another option than war... And we should pursue it until there is no more hope. 99
>
> *(President Jacques Chirac of France, March 16, 2003)*

The terms of Resolution 1441 strongly disapproved of the Iraqi government's actions. However it was deliberately phrased so that it could not be seen as justifying military action against Iraq unless another resolution specifically said this should happen. Iraq was instructed to produce within 30 days a document saying what it had done with its weapons, which it handed over on December 7, 2002. By then, however, the United States had decided that only military action could end what it said was the danger from Iraq. But UN backing for war could not be obtained, since France and Russia were unwilling to agree.

> 66 The war in Iraq is in danger of rocking global stability and the foundations of international law. 99
>
> *(President Vladimir Putin of Russia, March 28, 2003)*

The Invasion of Iraq

On March 17, 2003, U.S. President Bush made a speech giving Saddam Hussein 48 hours to leave the country, or war would begin. The UNMOVIC weapons inspectors left Iraq on March 18. On March 20 hostilities began, with an air attack on Baghdad. "Operation Iraqi Freedom," as the campaign was named, was under way.

The invading forces entered Iraq from Kuwait in the south. The Turkish government refused to allow a U.S. force to enter Iraq from the north. The early stages of the invasion did not go as quickly as planned. The Iraqi port of Umm Qasr, on Iraq's tiny coastline at the head of the Gulf, did not fall for a week. Units of the Iraqi army, though separated from each other, continued to fight the invasion, as did some armed civilians.

The superior firepower of the invading coalition troops meant they were soon victorious, however. Baghdad fell on April 9. On May 1 President Bush declared that the war was over. People in the northern Kurdish areas were happy. However most Iraqis were not openly enthusiastic. In other parts of the world, many people still thought the war was wrong.

> **" The Iraqi people tried but failed to remove Saddam Hussein for 35 years. It was a difficult task, and we thank the Americans. "**
>
> *(Sayyed Bashir al-Musawi, an Iraqi **cleric** in northern Baghdad, May 20, 2003)*

British soldiers check local people on the road to Basra.

IRAQI RESISTANCE

The Iraqi resistance included units of the regular army, as well as paramilitary forces. The Iraqi government had given weapons to Ba'athist supporters and other militias before the invasion. Many resistance fighters were killed, but there were few coalition casualties.

Chaos reigned for Iraqi civilians, and there were many civilian casualties. Law and order broke down, and kidnapping and score-settling soon began. Looting also broke out. Iraqi government offices were stripped, with little attempt by the coalition troops to protect them. The Iraqi Museum was looted, though it was later discovered that museum staff had successfully hidden many treasures. In addition, services such as electricity, water, and sewage disposal, which were already neglected by the Iraqi government during sanctions, became even worse.

> **It really hurts to see the lack of security. I don't see the British doing anything about it. There are far too many guns around.**
>
> *(Anonymous former Iraqi policeman, May 14, 2003)*

After the fall of Baghdad, many local people looted everything they could from government buildings.

Sunnis, Kurds, and Shi'ites

The aftermath of the invasion has drawn attention to the divisions between Iraq's different communities. Many people ask whether these communities can continue to live together, and whether they will be able to forge a new country out of the ruins of the old Iraq.

The main splits in Iraq are between the Kurds in the north, the Sunni Muslims in the center, and the Shi'ites in the south. This is simplified, since there are members of every community in every part of the country. In addition, between 5 and 10 percent of Iraqis belong to smaller groups, including Arab Christians.

> **❝ Each community will try to get as much power and territory as it can. ❞**
> *(Ayatollah Mohammed Taqi al-Muddaresi, a senior Shi'ite cleric)*

The Sunni Muslims have been the ruling group in Iraq for many years, as Saddam Hussein's supporters were a Sunni group. Sunnis make up only 20 percent of the Arab population of Iraq, however. Most of the Kurds are also Sunnis (with a few Shi'ites), but see themselves as separate from the Arabs.

Shi'ite Muslims in Baghdad in January 2004 show posters of their leader, Grand Ayatollah Ali al-Sistani.

Almost 60 percent of Iraqis are Shi'ite Muslims, like many people who live in neighboring Iran. The Shi'ites were expected to welcome the invasion, but they have been less satisfied than was anticipated. In the new Iraq, the Shi'ites want recognition for the fact that they are the majority. Many follow religious leaders, such as Ayatollah Ali al-Sistani, who has tried to ease the conflicts between the invading forces and Shi'ite Muslim groups. However some Shi'ites want the new Iraq to be a Muslim religious state. This would probably not fit in with the Western-style democracy desired by the United States and its allies.

Around 18 percent of Iraqis are Kurdish. The Kurds now fear that they may lose their autonomy. They would like to control the northern city of Kirkuk, which they think of as their capital, and to have part of Iraq's oil resources for themselves.

Kurdish demonstrators in the city of Kirkuk demand a federal state.

RIVAL VIEWPOINTS
Some Kurds demand a federal system of government in Iraq, in which regional assemblies would control each area. The Kurds have already experienced autonomy within Iraq, during the 12 years when Saddam Hussein was prevented from interfering in the Kurdish area.

In contrast the Shi'ites favor a single Arab state, which would give them a dominant position because they are the largest single group.

❝ We cannot take our proposal for autonomy to an Iraqi assembly. It would be killed off, because we are a minority. ❞
(Hoshyar Zebari, Iraqi foreign minister, who is a Kurd)

2003-2004: Resistance Continues

While most Iraqis were relieved that Saddam Hussein's government had been overthrown, resistance to the American forces carried on through 2003 and 2004. This was in spite of the fact that elections were due to take place in January 2005.

In May 2003 the occupying forces set up a body called the **Coalition Provisional Authority**, headed by Paul Bremer, an American **diplomat**. The Coalition Provisional Authority governed the country. The U.S. authorities also appointed an Iraqi advisory body, the Iraqi Governing Council.

However these political bodies could not stop the violence. Throughout 2003 and into 2004, attacks on the occupying forces became increasingly regular. According to the **interim** Iraqi authorities and U.S. officials, these attacks were the work of former Ba'athists, religious fanatics, and foreign fighters.

Some Iraqis condemned the continued violence. A large number of Iraqis, however, believed that the reason behind the attacks was the refusal of many people to tolerate continued foreign occupation. There were especially violent scenes in the Shi'ite holy city of Najaf and the Sunni stronghold of Fallujah.

IRAQI CASUALTIES
In October 2004 a study by U.S. scientists said that 100,000 Iraqis had died as a result of the war. Previous estimates of civilian deaths (from violence, not including disease and other health problems) had suggested a minimum figure of 15,000. Just over 1,000 U.S. soldiers had died in the same period.

❝ What they [the invading forces] have achieved is chaos, collective punishment, assassinations, the torture of prisoners, and the destruction of the country's infrastructure. **❞**
(Haifa Zangana, Iraqi-born novelist, October 25, 2004)

As the violence went on, Iraq's basic services such as electricity and water were not fully repaired. There was also widespread unemployment, while many people felt threatened by the increasing violence and lawlessness.

As time passed, the violence seemed only to intensify. There were kidnappings of Iraqis and foreigners, and some kidnap victims were killed. Suicide bombings began to be a daily event, and happened even next to the so-called Green Zone in Baghdad, where the Coalition Provisional Authority was based. Many of the Iraqis who were killed were those who had been cooperating with the U.S. forces, particularly recruits to the new police force. In December 2004 a suicide bomb at a U.S. base in Mosul killed 23 people, including 19 Americans.

> **" A free Iraq will be a decisive blow to terrorism and a victory for the civilized world and for the security of America. "**
> (President George W. Bush, June 1, 2004)

The horrendous aftermath of a suicide bombing in Najaf on December 20, 2004.

Interim Government

In the second half of 2004, Iraq entered a new phase. The U.S.-led occupying forces attempted to put a final end to resistance and violence in the country, in preparation for elections in January 2005. The first step was to give more power to Iraqis.

On June 1, 2004 the Coalition Provisional Authority ceased to exist. An assembly of 1,000 influential Iraqis then chose the members of the Iraqi Interim Government. This new government, in theory, now ruled over Iraq. Dr. Ayad Allawi, a Shi'ite, became the interim prime minister.

American officials continued to be closely involved in the running of the country. The American forces consulted with the Iraqi Interim Government, but they did not take direct orders from it.

AYAD ALLAWI

Dr. Ayad Allawi, Iraq's interim prime minister, was born in 1945. As a young man, he joined the Ba'ath Party. In 1971 he moved to London to continue his medical studies, and resigned from the Ba'ath in 1975. In 1978 an attempt was made to murder him. In 1990 he founded an Iraqi opposition group in exile called the Iraqi National Accord. He had links with the intelligence services in Great Britain and the United States.

Dr. Ayad Allawi (left), the interim prime minister of Iraq, with U.S. President George W. Bush at the White House in 2004.

Security continued to be a problem. The U.S. occupying forces fired all Ba'ath Party members, so the government had to rely on inexperienced police recruits. These new recruits were regularly attacked by forces opposed to the invasion of Iraq and many were killed in car bombings and other attacks. Some former Ba'athists were later allowed to work for the new authorities.

Meanwhile temporary solutions were found to some security problems. Shi'ite violence in the holy city of Najaf was stopped after an agreement was reached with Shi'ite leader Moqtada al-Sadr. Violence in Sadr City, the Shi'ite suburb of Baghdad, was also brought to an end. The U.S. military and the Interim Government also agreed on the need to halt Sunni resistance in Fallujah. American officials said the order for an assault on Fallujah had to come from the Iraqis. The attack on Fallujah began in November 2004.

> " The terrorists and **insurgents** continue to use Fallujah and the Fallujah people as a shield for their murderous acts... I cannot stand back and allow such attacks to continue. "
> (Iraqi interim Prime Minister Dr. Ayad Allawi, October 2004)

This masked militia man holds a rocket brought into an army post in the Shi'ite Baghdad suburb known as Sadr City, in response to the Interim Government's call for an arms amnesty.

Turbulent Iraq

Iraq's future depends on its security. Unless the violence in Iraq ends, it will be difficult for the oil industry to recover. Without the income from oil, the government will find it hard to get Iraq's schools, hospitals, roads, and railways working again.

There are some good things about Iraq's situation. Few people miss Saddam Hussein. The country is on the road to democracy. However many blame the occupying forces for the continuing violence and civilian deaths. The United States hoped that, following Iraq's democratic elections of 2005, violence would decrease, but this did not happen immediately.

One ongoing problem is that few Sunni Muslims have become involved in the new government of Iraq. Many of Saddam's supporters were Sunnis, and their dislike of the Shi'ite majority meant that many refused to vote in 2005. Instead, Sunni terrorists have launched suicide bombings, and regular kidnappings and murders of civilians. The terrorists have also targeted Iraq's new police force, with many recruits and officers being killed.

An Iraqi protests against the kidnapping of aid worker Margaret Hassan in October 2004. Mrs. Hassan, who had lived in Iraq for 30 years and was married to an Iraqi, was murdered shortly after.

❝ While there is no single root cause of terrorism, perceived humiliation and a lack of political and economic opportunities make young men susceptible to extremism. This can evolve easily into violence. ❞
(Harvard University terrorism expert Jessica Stern)

Iraqis in Najaf wave their voting registration papers. The election for the Transitional National Assembly was held on January 30, 2005. Shi'ites gained the most votes.

Without an effective police force, recovery and democracy will be extremely difficult for Iraq. In each bombing incident, many of the dead are recruits to Iraq's new security forces, but most are innocent civilians. Kidnappings by criminals are common. Many Iraqis who can afford to are leaving the country, especially Iraq's Christians.

Iraq's economy suffered because of the old UN sanctions regime, and continues to struggle today. By 2003 work and business had virtually stopped. Though there was some recovery after the invasion, unemployment was still widespread and pay was low. Iraq's oil industry continued to run at a reduced level, and there were regular attacks on the oil pipelines. The recovery of Iraq looks like being a long and difficult process.

" Civilian deaths have always been a tragic reality of modern war. But the conflict in Iraq was supposed to be different... U.S. and British forces were dispatched to liberate the Iraqi people, not to impose their own tyranny of violence. "
(Scott Ritter, former UN weapons inspector, and U.S. marine)

Glossary

Abbasid dynasty dynasty of Caliphs who ruled in Baghdad from 749 C.E. to 1258 C.E.

aggression attacking something or someone for no reason

autonomous, autonomy having self government, but in general within another country rather than in a separate state

Ba'ath Party non-religious political party founded in Syria in the 1940s, but also strong in Iraq. It is based on Arab nationalism and socialism. Ba'athism's founder, Michael Aflaq, was a Christian. Both Muslims and Christians have been Ba'athists. Unfortunately, Ba'athist governments have always been led by dictators.

Ba'athists Ba'ath means rebirth. Ba'athists are members of the Ba'ath Party.

biological weapons weapons that cause harm by releasing dangerous germs or viruses

Caliph successor to the Prophet Mohammed as the leader of the Muslim community. There is no Caliph today.

ceasefire when fighting nations or groups agree to momentarily stop fighting

chemical weapons weapons that cause harm by releasing dangerous chemicals. Modern chemical weapons damage a victim's nervous system, causing rapid death.

child mortality rate number of children who die, normally expressed as the number of deaths per 1,000 live births

cleric minister of religion. In Islam clerics have no particular ceremony in which they become men of God. They reach their position through devotion to God and learning, causing other clerics and ordinary people to accept them.

coalition when countries work together to achieve a common goal

Coalition Provisional Authority government body set up in 2003 by the victorious allies, led by the United States, to govern Iraq

communist person who believes in a system of government in which a single party controls everything and there is no private property

Constantinople name of the great city that was the capital of the Roman Empire of the East. The Greeks called it Byzantium and the Turks renamed it Istanbul, which is its modern name.

constitution document containing all the legal rules under which a country is governed. A constitution also sets out the powers of the different parts of the government in relation to each other.

coup violent action that leads to a change in government. Coups are mainly, but not always, carried out by the military.

democracy system in which the people of a country hold elections to choose who their government leaders will be. In a democratic country, there is also in general what is known as the rule of law. This means the government cannot do what it likes, but must obey the laws.

dictator ruler who orders people to do what he wishes, and does not consult the people about what they want

diplomat person who works out and negotiates issues between nations

inflation when a country's currency loses its value, and more money is needed to buy goods. If wages do not rise, people become poorer.

insurgent person who tries to overthrow an established government by violence, for whatever reason

interim refers to something temporary, meant only for a limited time rather than permanently

irrigating, irrigation to supply land with water by artificial means

Kurds people who live mainly in northern Iraq and some other surrounding countries. They are a minority in Iraq.

latitude horizontal lines around the earth specified by a number of degrees north or south of the Equator

mandate arrangement where a developed country became a kind of caretaker, looking after a new country until it was supposedly ready for independence

Mesopotamia old name for what became Iraq. It means "the land between the rivers."

minorities small parts of a population that differ from the main part (majority) in some characteristics. Minorities are sometimes treated badly by the majority.

nationalist member of a political party or group who wants an independent nation

neo-conservative refers to a number of U.S. foreign policy advisers who favor an active American foreign policy intended to spread democracy and pro-American attitudes in the world by whatever means necessary

oil reserves the total amount of oil that a country has that is still in the ground

Ottoman Empire Turkish Empire that dominated the Middle East for four centuries until its disappearance at the end of World War I

province separate district or area of a country

regent person who holds royal power temporarily while waiting for an infant monarch to become an adult. Iraq had a regent from 1939 to 1953.

regime government in power

Revolutionary Command Council (RCC) expression used to describe a group of senior officers who help govern a country where the president has come to power in a military coup. General Qassem appointed an RCC in Iraq, and there continued to be an RCC under Saddam Hussein.

sanctions form of punishment, where the United Nations bans a country from trading or from other activities in order to force it to obey a UN resolution

Security Council resolution formal decision to take action against a nation or group that is breaking international law. It is voted on by the UN Security Council (see United Nations).

Shi'ite Muslims members of the Shi'a sect of Islam. 60 percent of Iraqis are Shi'ites (see Sunni Muslims).

subsidies money given to a person, company, or nation to assist in an activity that is good for the general public

Sunni Muslims the split between Sunni and Shi'ite dates back to the early days of Islam, when the Prophet's cousin and son-in-law, Ali, challenged Mu'awiya for the position of Caliph. The Sunnis were the mainstream, while the Shi'ites, who followed Ali, believed a Caliph should be a descendant of Mohammed. The Sunnis and Shi'ites have different religious practices, but both stand by the basic principles of Islam.

Taliban hardline Sunni Muslim rulers of Afghanistan. They were overthrown in December 2001.

United Nations (UN) all countries are members of this organization. Its job is to try to keep the peace in the world. The body within the UN that passes resolutions that members must obey is called the Security Council. The Security Council has fifteen members. Five of these (the United States, Great Britain, France, Russia, and China) are permanent members. The other ten members are taken from the entire membership of the United Nations, with each country serving for a two-year period.

weapons of mass destruction (WMD) normally means nuclear, chemical, and biological weapons, used to kill as many people as possible at once

Facts and Figures

IRAQ

GEOGRAPHY

Location: Middle East, bordering the Gulf, west of Iran

Area: 168,000 square miles (437,072 square kilometers). This is slightly more than twice the size of Idaho, and 20 percent smaller than France.

Land borders: Jordan, Syria, Turkey, Iran, Kuwait, and Saudi Arabia

Climate: Extreme. Winter is cool in the south, harsh in the north. Summer temperatures in the south can rise extremely high to over 120 °F.

Land use:

Arable land	14 percent
Uncultivated	86 percent

The land is mainly desert.

POPULATION

Population size: 26,074,906

Age structure:

0–14 years	40 percent
15–64 years	57 percent
65 years and above	3 percent

Median age: 19.4 years

Population growth rate: 2.7 percent

Life expectancy at birth:

Total population	68.7 years
Male	67.5 years
Female	70.0 years

Ethnic groups:

Arabs	75–80 percent
Kurds	15–20 percent
Others	5 percent

Religions:

Muslim	97 percent
(consisting of Shi'ite	60–65 percent
and Sunni	32–37 percent)
Christian and other	3 percent

Literacy rate (age 15 years and over):

Total population	40 percent
Male	56 percent
Female	24 percent

ECONOMY

Iraq's economy depends on oil, which has traditionally provided 95 percent of Iraq's foreign earnings. International sanctions since 1991 have severely limited Iraq's earnings from this source and the oil infrastructure has been damaged since the U.S.-led invasion in 2003. Rebuilding of oil, electricity, and other infrastructure is under way, but is hampered by the insurgency.

GDP: $89.8 billion

GDP growth rate: 52.3 percent

GDP per capita (at purchasing power parity): $3,500
This figure means that the GDP per capita in Iraq in local currency would buy the same quantity of goods as would $3,500 spent in the United States.

GDP by sector:

Agriculture	13.6 percent
Industry	58.6 percent
Services	27.8 percent

Oil production: 2.25 million barrels per day
Pre-war production under sanctions restrictions (2002) was 2.8 million barrels per day.

Oil reserves: 112.5 billion barrels

Inflation rate: 25.4 percent

Labor force: 6.7 million
A post-war economic shutdown in many sectors in Iraq means that unemployment remains very high at the moment.

(*Source:* CIA World Factbook, 2005)

Timelines

1910–1990 C.E.

1910

1917 British troops occupy Baghdad

1920
1920 League of Nations Mandate over Iraq given to Great Britain. Anti-British uprising.
1921 Faisal I becomes King

1930
1932 Iraq becomes independent, signs treaty with Britain
1933 King Ghazi takes the throne
1937 Saddam Hussein born in Tikrit
1939 Death of King Ghazi, succeeded by King Faisal II (aged 4)
1940
1941 Coup by Rashid Ali Gailani, overthrown by return of British forces

1945 Iraq joins Arab League

1948 Iraq takes part in fight against Israel
1950

1953 Faisal II begins his rule
1955 Iraq signs Baghdad Pact alliance

1960
1958 Iraqi government overthrown by military coup led by General Qassem. King Faisal II is killed, with other leading figures.

1963 First Ba'ath Party coup by Colonel Arif. General Qassem executed.

1968 Second Ba'athist coup brings President Bakr to power
1970

1979 Saddam Hussein takes over from Bakr
1980
1980 Iran-Iraq war begins

1988 Saddam Hussein attacks the Kurds with chemical weapons in Halabja
1988 Iran-Iraq war ends
1990

1990–2005 C.E.

1990
1990 Aug. 2: Iraq invades Kuwait
Aug. 6: United Nations imposes first sanctions on Iraq
1991 Jan. 16: Gulf War begins with air strikes on Iraq
Feb. 27: U.S.-led alliance drives Iraqi troops out of Kuwait
Mar. 3: Iraq accepts ceasefire
Apr. 6: Iraq accepts UN resolution, setting up weapons inspections to make sure it has destroyed its banned weapons
Apr. 10: "Safe haven" established in northern Iraq for the Kurds
1992 Apr. 26: United States and Britain establish no-fly zone in southern Iraq

1995
1995 Apr. 14: UN Oil-for-Food Program begins, enabling Iraq to sell oil to buy food and medicine

1998 Dec. 13: Iraq first withdraws cooperation from UN inspectors.
Dec. 16: UN inspectors withdraw
2000
from Iraq and Operation Desert Fox begins, when the United States and Britain bomb Iraqi targets

2001
2001 Feb. 15: More air attacks on Iraq after Iraq air defenses threaten British and U.S. planes

2002
2002 Jan. 30: U.S. President George W. Bush says Iraq is part of Axis of Evil
Nov. 27: UN weapons inspectors return to Iraq
Dec. 19: United States says Iraq is going against United Nations resolutions on disarmament
2003
2003 Mar. 20: War starts in Iraq with invasion by U.S. and British troops
Apr. 9: Baghdad is captured
Dec. 13: Saddam Hussein is captured

2004
2004 Jun. 28: Interim Government set up under Prime Minister Ayad Allawi

2005 Jan. 30: Iraq holds first free elections
2005
Apr. 6: Interim Iraqi government elects first Kurdish president, Jalal Talabani

51

Who's Who?

Abdullah Born in 1912, and murdered in 1958. Prince Abdullah was the Prince Regent of Iraq from 1939 to 1953, while his nephew King Faisal II was a minor. He then became Crown Prince from 1953 until his death in 1958. Abullah was a strong figure in Iraq and remained influential in government even after King Faisal II became king in 1953.

Aflaq, Michael Born in 1910 and died in 1989. Aflaq was a Syrian intellectual and teacher who founded the Ba'ath Party. He was a Christian who studied in Paris. Aflaq became a full-time political activist in 1942. He moved to Baghdad after the Ba'athist coup there in 1968.

Alexander the Great Lived from 356 B.C.E. to 323 B.C.E. Alexander was a Macedonian King from northern Greece whose brilliant military successes enabled him to conquer neighboring countries. His Empire eventually extended over much of what was then the known world, including Iraq. He ruled countries from Egypt to India, where he set up members of his circle as kings.

Allawi, Ayad Born in 1945. Allawi qualified as a doctor at Baghdad University and joined the Ba'ath Party. He left Iraq in 1971 and continued his medical career in Great Britain, where he specialized as a neurologist and then became a businessman. Allawi left the Ba'ath Party in 1975, and survived an assassination attempt in 1978. Dr. Allawi was known to both British and U.S. intelligence as an Iraqi opposition leader. He returned to Iraq in 2003. Allawi was chosen as a member of the Interim Governing Council, and became prime minister of the interim government in May 2004. In the Iraqi elections of January 30, 2005, Allawi's party won only 40 of 275 seats. He remained as prime minister until Ibrahim Jaafari, leader of the Shi'ite United Iraqi Alliance, succeeded him on April 28, 2005.

al-Said, Nuri Born in 1888 and murdered in 1958. Nuri al-Said began his career as a soldier and became Iraq's chief of staff under King Faisal I. Al-Said became prime minister for the first time in 1930. He played a leading role in Iraq as a supporter of the monarchy. He was prime minister at the time of the military coup in 1958, when he was killed.

Arif, Abdel-Salam Born in 1920 and died in 1966. He was a career soldier who was president of Iraq from 1963 to 1966. He was killed in a helicopter accident, and was succeeded as president by his brother, Abdel Rahman Aref.

Bakr, Hassan Born in 1912, and died in 1982. President Bakr was a professional soldier who led the Ba'athist coup in Iraq in 1968. Saddam Hussein, who was a distant relative, was his security chief and became his right-hand man. Bakr resigned from his post in 1979 to allow Saddam Hussein to take over.

Bin Laden, Osama Born in 1957 into a rich Saudi family. Bin Laden's father made a large fortune as a civil engineer, constructing buildings in Saudi Arabia and elsewhere in the Middle East. Bin Laden came under the influence of Islamic extremists while he was a student and went to Afghanistan to fight the occupying Soviet forces in 1979. He became a leader of the Islamic extremist group opposed to all influence in the Middle East by the United States, and his organization, known as Al-Qaeda, approved, funded, and helped to plan the September 11 attacks on the United States. Following the overthrow of the Taliban regime in Afghanistan in 2001, bin Laden remained unfound.

Blair, Tony Born in 1953. Prime minister of Great Britain from 1997. Blair trained as a lawyer, and later joined the Labour Party. He was first elected as a member of the British parliament in 1983 and became prime minister in 1997. Blair sent British troops to aid the U.S.-led invasion of Iraq in 2003.

Bremer, Paul Born in 1941. Bremer is a career diplomat and former ambassador who became administrator of the Coalition Provisional Authority in Iraq in May 2003. He handed control over to the Interim Government in Iraq in June 2004.

Bush, George H. W. 41st President of the United States (1989–1993). Bush was born in 1924. He formed an alliance to drive Iraq's troops out of Kuwait in 1991.

Bush, George W. 43rd President of the United States (2001–due to leave office in 2009). Bush was born in 1946. He made the decision to invade Iraq in March 2003.

Cheney, Dick Born in 1941. Cheney has served under several Republican presidents in administrative posts and also made a success of his business career. He became a congressman in 1978, and then defense secretary under the first President Bush in 1989. He then became chairman and CEO of Halliburton Corporation in 1995. Cheney became vice president in 2001.

Chirac, Jacques Born in 1932. After studying political science and administration, including a period at Harvard University, Chirac joined the staff of President Pompidou in 1962. He became a member of the National Assembly in 1967, as a member of a right-wing, conservative party. He served twice as prime minister and became president of France, after his third attempt, in 1995.

Clinton, William (Bill) 42nd President of the United States (1993–2001). Clinton was born in 1946. He launched an air attack on Iraq in 1998.

Faisal I Born in 1885, and died in 1933. King Faisal I was one of the sons of Hussein ibn Ali, the Sherif of Mecca, who led the Arab Revolt against the Turks in World War I. Faisal I became king of Iraq in 1921.

Faisal II Born in 1935 and murdered in 1958. King Faisal II was an infant when he became king of Iraq after his father died. His uncle Prince Abdullah ruled as Regent until 1953, when King Faisal II reached the legal age to become king. He was murdered along with other members of the royal family and politicians in 1958 when a military coup overthrew the monarchy in Iraq.

Ghazi, King Born in 1912, he died in a car accident in 1939. Ghazi succeeded King Faisal I as King of Iraq.

Hammurabi Lived from around 1792 to 1750 B.C.E. Hammurabi was a Babylonian king who ruled Iraq. He issued an important legal code and ruled over a well-organized kingdom.

Hulagu Lived from 1217 to 1265 C.E. Hulagu was the Mongol ruler Genghis Khan's grandson. Hulagu conquered western Asia and parts of the Middle East, including Iraq, ending the Abbasid Caliphate.

Hussein, Saddam Born in 1937. Saddam Hussein is the former president of Iraq. He rose to power through the Iraqi Ba'ath Party. He was responsible for Iraq's eight-year war with Iran from 1980 to 1988 and then for the Iraqi invasion of Kuwait in 1990. The United States and other Western countries suspected that he was not obeying the United Nations resolution telling him to get rid of his weapons of mass destruction. This led to the U.S.-led invasion of Iraq in 2003. Hussein was captured by Coalition troops in December 2003.

Lawrence, T.E. ("Lawrence of Arabia") Born in 1888, died in 1935. Lawrence was an Oxford scholar and British army officer. He fought in the Middle East in World War I in the Arab Revolt against the Turks.

Mohammed Born in 570 C.E., and died in 632 C.E. In around 610 C.E., the Prophet Mohammed claimed to receive the text of the Qur'an from the Angel Gabriel who appeared to him. Mohammed founded the Islamic faith and led a growing community of Muslims in the Middle East.

Nasser, Gamal Abdul President Nasser of Egypt was born in 1918 and died in 1970. As a young officer, he was the leader of the Egyptian Revolution in 1952. He became president of Egypt in 1954. He was much admired throughout the Arab world, including Iraq. He died of heart disease in 1970.

Putin, Vladimir Born in 1952. Putin studied law in Leningrad and worked in Soviet intelligence from 1975. Between 1985 and 1990, he worked in East Germany. He then worked in various political administrative positions in Russia, and became intelligence chief again under President Yeltsin in 1998. Yeltsin made Putin prime minister in 1999. Putin was elected president of Russia in 2000.

Qassem, Abdul Karim Born in 1914, and murdered in 1963. Qassem was a professional soldier who rose through the ranks and then led the military coup in Iraq in 1958. Egypt's President Nasser was his inspiration, but he was primarily an Iraqi nationalist who believed the country was being ruined by the monarchy and the politicians who surrounded the king. President Qassem was killed in the Ba'athist coup in 1963.

Rumsfeld, Donald Born in 1923. Rumsfeld became U.S. Secretary of Defense in 2001. A former congressman, he has served in numerous posts in Republican administrations. He is regarded as part of the circle surrounding President George W. Bush who favored the armed invasion of Iraq. He has also had a successful business career.

Schwarzkopf, General Norman Born in 1934. General Schwarzkopf was Allied commander in the Gulf War of 1990–1991. Schwarzkopf is a career soldier in the U.S. Army who also served in Vietnam.

Find Out More

BOOKS FOR YOUNGER READERS

King, John. *The Invasion of Kuwait*. Chicago: Raintree, 2003.
An account of Iraq's invasion of Kuwait in 1990 and the reaction to it around the world.

Nakaya, Andrea C. *Iraq*. San Diego: Greenhaven Press, 2004.
A good source of information on the history of Iraq.

Torr, James D. *Weapons of Mass Destruction*. San Diego: Greenhaven Press, 2004.
Looks at what weapons of mass destruction are and how can they be stopped.

BOOKS FOR OLDER READERS

Dabrowska, Karen. *Iraq: the Bradt Travel Guide*. Guilford: Globe Pequot Press, 2002.
A guide book to Iraq by an author who traveled to the country to explore the possibilities for tourism and who is a careful and fair observer.

Hiro, Dilip. *Iraq: a Report from the Inside*. New York: Granta Books, 2003.
Insights into the country from an expert author.

Keegan, John. *The Iraq War*. New York: Knopf, 2004.
A very informative book about the Gulf War of 2003, by a respected military historian.

Tripp, Charles. *Iraq*. New York: Cambridge University Press, 2002.
An excellent general history of Iraq.

ADDRESSES TO WRITE TO

If you want to find out more about Iraq, try contacting these organizations:

Middle East Institute
1761 N. Street, N.W.
Washington, D.C. 20036-2882

The Brookings Institution
1775 Massachusetts Avenue, N.W.
Washington, D.C. 20036-2188

Center for Strategic and International Studies
800 K Street, N.W.
Washington, D.C. 20006

Washington Report on Middle East Affairs
American Educational Trust, Inc.
P.O. Box 53062
Washington, D.C. 20009

Index

Numbers in *italics* refer to captions to illustrations

Index